FASHIONS OF A DECADE
THE
1920s

FASHIONS OF A DECADE

THE 1920s

Jacqueline Herald

Series Editors: Valerie Cumming and Elane Feldman
Original Illustrations by Robert Price

B. T. Batsford Ltd · London

Contents

THE 1920s (FASHIONS OF A DECADE SERIES)

Text design by David Stanley
Jacket design by Sue Lacey
Composition by Latimer Trend
Manufactured by Bookbuilders Ltd
Printed in Hong Kong

For the publishers:
B.T. Batsford Ltd
4 Fitzhardinge Street
London W1H 0AH

ISBN 07134 6638 3
A CIP catalogue record for this book
is available from the British Library.

THE 20s

This was the Jazz Age, the decade of the flappers – as they were called in the United States – known in Britain as Bright Young Things. The 1920s opened with an explosion of colour and the wailing sounds and fast rhythms of jazz and energetic dancing. It was a period of escapism, a youthful reaction against the dark and serious clothes, behaviour and mood of an older generation that was still clinging to old Victorian and Edwardian values. To the enthusiastic lyrics of "Everybody's Doing It Now", the new society hurtled through the twenties at an optimistic pace. Suddenly the world seemed smaller. Internationalism – a move toward breaking down national limits in many fields, including finance and style – was a theme that ran through the decade. Above all, it was an attitude, but new links were made possible through developments in transport. Motor racing was a popular spectator sport, and happy family motoring was enjoyed by many – thanks to Henry Ford's assembly line. Ford was enormously successful in catering to a mass market through his modern system of production, in which a series of workers and their apparatus worked at the pace of the moving assembly line, each worker adding one component in a systematic conveyor-belt type of production. This is how Ford's famous model T car – a standard design, made of interchangeable parts – was put together. In Britain, too, more cars appeared on the road, necessitating the first traffic lights in 1928. Passenger air travel began in the mid-twenties, though fashionable people with time on their hands cruised at a more leisurely pace in expensively furnished private yachts and large ocean liners.

Radio Concerts

In June 1920 the nightingale voice of Australian prima donna Dame Nellie Melba sang "Addio" from *La Bohème* in a radio concert that launched public broadcasting in Britain, but radio stations were scattered irregularly around the nation, limiting the number of households that could "tune in". However, public broadcasts in the United States were much more regular and widespread, following the opening of thousands of commercial radio stations. As more and more people began to enjoy broadcast music, their taste for jazz and new melodies became more diverse. On the negative side, instant rhythms at the turn of a knob (or, for that matter, the winding up of a 78 r.p.m. gramophone) caused a decline in singing and piano playing at home and a steady reduction in the number of music and singing teachers. However, few working-class homes in the 1920s could afford the cost of a radio.

Compared to the United States, industrial expansion in Europe was slow.

Egyptian-inspired accessories – tiny combs for short hair, powder compact, cigarette case and pendant.

Mass manufacture using standardized parts (known as the "American system" of production) was well under way in the United States. However, European nations were still repaying the loans taken out to finance World War I, and so had limited funds to invest in industry.

In terms of fashion and behaviour, the 1920s appeared to be a decade of fun for the consumer; but beneath this jazzed-up facade, there were all kinds of social and moral tensions. In America, despite a growth of interest in fundamentalist Christian religions and despite the Federal Volstead Act of 1919 prohibiting the sale but not the consumption of alcohol, there was a huge increase in the illegal smuggling, manufacturing and selling of what was called "bootleg whiskey".

Gangsters cashed in on this new "business". Chicago's Al Capone was one of the era's most notorious gangsters. His activities drew the kind of media attention that was previously reserved for foreign royalty and dignitaries, or American politicians and celebrities.

The fact that so many Americans were drinking illegally during Prohibition, whether at home or in clubs (called "speakeasies"), bred a climate of acceptance of certain types of criminal behaviour. This loosening of moral standards had a widespread impact on many people's approach to life.

The original Charleston from *Runnin' Wild.* A sheet music cover of 1923.

Crossword puzzle stockings were a craze of 1925.

Showing One's Colours

Some aspects of pre-war fashion were rebelled against; others – like driving hats and veils – took on a new inspirational role. Wartime garments also adopted a new look. Some men's garments (knitted cardigans, for example) were translated into women's fashions. The practicality of the weatherproofed gabardine Burberry raincoat ensured that it would become an international classic of the future for men and women alike. Leather helmets, jackets and coats entered fast-moving sportswear, being worn for flying and driving. The heroine of Michael Arlen's novel *The Green Hat*, Iris Storm (based on the writer and campaigner for black causes, Nancy Cunard), wore one. However, during the decade leather became associated with the military-style uniforms of the Nazi party, which was rising in popularity in the twenties. (The Nazis were one of several extremist-right-wing German nationalist groups protesting against the collapse of the Deutschmark in 1923.) The SA (storm troopers) wore over-the-knee leather "jackboots" with their brown uniforms and armbands displaying the party symbol, the swastika.

Meanwhile in 1922, Benito Mussolini had become Europe's first Fascist dictator and Italy's prime minister. In what became known as the "top hat revolution", Mussolini marched into Rome with his 22,000 black-shirted supporters who called him "Il Duce" (The Leader). Once in power, he continued to wear black, but insisted on distinguishing himself by wearing a silk top hat. The Italians were the first to adopt Fascism, a system of nationalist and anti-Communist dictatorship. Fascism was most successful in countries like Italy and Germany, where high unemployment, extreme poverty and low morale made people more easily convinced by the promises of the would-be dictators to make their countries great again.

While black was the colour of Fascism, green was the symbol of pacifism. White, on the other hand, was the colour of the long robes and hoods with narrow eye-slits worn by the members of America's Ku Klux Klan, a fanatical, racially and religiously intolerant organization originally founded in 1865, and revived in the twenties. It was also the colour of *khadi*, a humble hand-spun, hand-woven indigenous cotton cloth worn by India's Mohandas K. (Mahatma) Gandhi as an anti-British gesture, for which he was imprisoned in 1922. To Gandhi, tailored clothes and the cotton manufactured in the mills of Manchester in England represented political oppression, from which his country was seeking independence. By contrast, Turkey's president Mustafa Kemal (Atatürk) looked on Western clothing as an essential part of his country's modernization programme. He made wearing the fez – the men's hat that symbolized Islamic orthodoxy – a criminal offence, and also discouraged women from wearing the face-covering veil of traditional Islam.

In the USSR, photographer Alexander

Motoring fashions worn at a motor racing meeting, France 1923. The leather jackets, coats and helmets are worn with goggles – the colourful bohemian-like scarves are casually worn about the neck.

Charles Lindbergh, the American aviator, who made the first solo transatlantic flight in 1927.

Rodchenko developed a revolutionary kind of clothing for men, based on a boiler suit and worn with a flat cap. The Communist ideology of power lying with the workers was reflected by Rodchenko's fashion idea, which represented the Soviet hope of an egalitarian future.

Tutankhamen's Tomb discovered near Thebes

In 1922 Howard Carter, a British archaeologist, discovered the rich treasures of the Egyptian boy king Tutankhamen, which had been buried for more than 3000 years. The world's press attempted desperately to get a photograph of the site, but as the excavations were shrouded in secrecy until the following year, the whole discovery fired public imagination and erupted in an explosion of "Tutmania" – a whole range of fashions and objects were decorated in Egyptian motifs and colours. The new fashion shades were christened with exotic names like Coptic blue, lotus, sakkara, mummy brown and carnelian.

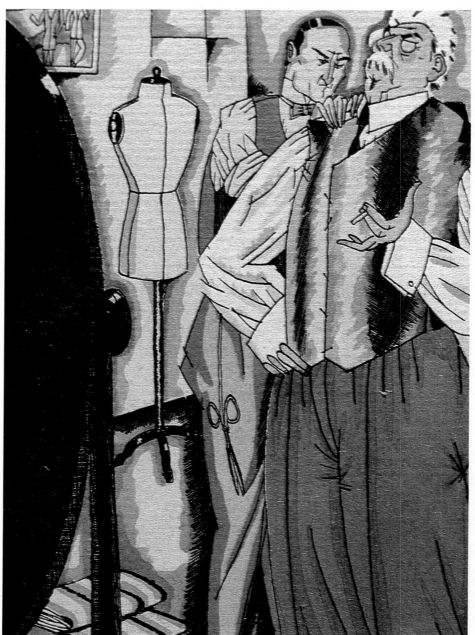

Ascot fashions of 1929.

Fitting at the tailor's.

The Social Calendar

Though the phrase the "New Poor" was heard more and more frequently – in Europe at least – upper-class society operated according to the pre-war social calendar. This pattern of events is what the top end of the fashion industry was built on. Spring-summer collections of model clothes were launched by the fashion houses in time for the new "season". This included grand balls, visits to the races (for example, Ascot in England, Longchamps in France or, in America, Saratoga), garden parties and the attendance of private views of exhibitions of art. By July society moved to the country, or to the new resorts on the French Riviera or Palm Beach, Florida. Autumn was devoted to hunting and shooting – in Scotland, for instance – and the great cities of London, New York, Paris and Rome were the places to return to for the winter.

Social convention demanded that clothes be appropriate for the time of day, the activity or the formality of the occasion. Even servants such as housemaids were required to follow suit, and had morning and afternoon uniforms. Generally, the higher someone was ranked socially, the more clothes were needed to meet these demands and to impress. In England, to keep up appearances, an annual dress allowance might be given to a daughter when she married, as part of her dowry settlement.

Postwar Emancipation for Women

The devastating loss of so many men in World War I meant that the female population in much of Europe outnumbered the male. In 1918 the British fight for votes for women secured a major victory when Parliament passed the Representation of the People Bill. However, it only applied to women over 30. The United States Constitution's 19th Amendment of 1920 enfranchised American women. And throughout the decade, a number of new laws helped to change women's status in society. Though the number of female undergraduates was still much lower than that of men, women were beginning to enter male-dominated professions, but not without a battle. The exception was in the office, where male clerks were generally being replaced by women typists and secretaries. Although female doctors were still rare, birth control pioneers Margaret Sanger and Dr Marie Stopes founded their first clinics in New York and London, respectively.

The passport for social success was wealth or marriage into the nobility. This is what Hollywood's Gloria Swanson did. Having secured her marriage to the marquis de la Falaise de Coudray, a "docile nobleman with a reckless taste in spats", she was attended in her grand mansion by servants who wore eighteenth-century-style powdered wigs and satin knee breeches.

Encounter on a staircase at a fashionable party.

French fashion designer Gabrielle (Coco) Chanel's success might never have happened without the financial backing of her rich lover; but, perhaps because of her poor and unconventional background, she was not afraid to shatter the formality of Paris's

Ritz Hotel by introducing the "Apache" sweater – a casual sweater, strikingly patterned with American Indian-type motifs. The important French fashion designer Paul Poiret, one of Chanel's rivals, accused her of making duchesses look like shopgirls and joked that her fashions represented a "pauvreté de luxe" (luxurious poverty – in other words, poverty for the rich!).

Taking a walk at Montmartre, Paris, in stormy shades of purple and shocking pink by the fashion house of Beer, 1920.

The Haute Couture Business

Initially, after World War I, there was a shortage of materials and skill with which to revitalize France's haute couture industry, the most expensive sector of the fashion industry. In the 1920s, since so many jobs in France depended on haute couture and the French reputation for fashion was so high, the French government encouraged banks to grant extended loans to the fashion trade. In order to monitor the working conditions of staff and to maintain high standards of workman-

ship, a professional association of Paris-based couturiers, the Chambre Syndicale de la Haute Couture Française, was established. As the market became more secure, the fashion industry grew rapidly, so that by 1927 it boasted 250,000 employees in Paris, distributed between the city's 2000 workrooms, salons and shops. But the Wall Street Crash of 1929 was a bad time for the trade, when suddenly 10,000 Parisians in the industry were unemployed.

Paris Exhibition

The term Art Deco was coined from the *Exposition des Arts Décoratifs et Industriels Modernes* ('Exhibition of Modern Decorative and Industrial Arts'), held in Paris in 1925. A series of pavilions displayed an international selection of design talent and industry. Above all, France's lead in the field of haute couture was celebrated in two sections devoted to fashion, Le Grand Palais and Le Pavilion d'Elégance. The latter was decorated by couturière Jeanne Lanvin, and showed the work of more than 60 couturiers. The jury's report on fashion in the exhibition was functionalism by day, fantasy by night. Amid sumptuous lacquer screens by Jean Dunand and the stylish bronze furniture of sculptor Armand Rateau, high-fashion clothes were displayed on ultra-modern forms designed by the sculptor Vigneau-Siégal. They were coloured olive green, purple, gold, silver or black – or left as natural wood.

By the 1920s, the structure of an haute couture fashion house fell into the following general pattern. One or two main salons were devoted to showing the season's collections of "model" garments. These were the prototypes, which were modelled by live models (known as "mannequins" in the 1920s) who paraded through the salon in front of the clients. The choice of mannequin was vital to secure a sale; in the mid-twenties, Jean Patou employed around 32 mannequins to model the 450 dresses making up each collection, six of whom had tall "American" figures.

Haute couture was so expensive and exclusive because the clothes were based directly on these "model" garments and made specially to order. The client would choose a design, and then be fitted for a copy of the model garment, to be made up in the fabric and colour of her choice. She would be attended to personally, always by the same *vendeuse* (saleswoman) and a fitter, both of whom would develop an intimate knowledge of her taste, figure and so forth. The *vendeuse* coordinated the whole order, from the choice of model gown or outfit, through three or more fittings, to the final delivery. She was assisted by a *seconde vendeuse*, who saw that all the details were completed according to the client's wishes. The fitter gave instructions to the *première main qualifiée*, the more senior of the two qualified seamstresses, who were assisted by an *arpette*, an apprentice whose lowly job was to pick up the pins. In addition, the house had a buyer, who was responsible for the purchase of materials, from bolts of luxurious fabrics of all kinds to notions, such as beads, sequins and feathers.

Members of royalty were permitted exclusivity on their selections – i.e., the particular design chosen would be withdrawn, so that nobody else could order a copy. And so the fashion house offered a very special service to customers who had the time – and money – to attend so many fittings. Though only a small proportion had access to this fashion, through magazine features the great fashion houses influenced what everybody else aspired to. And although designs could be protected by copyright, it was difficult to stop the "pirating" of

diluted or minimally changed forms by large-scale clothing manufacturers. The pirating of styles led to a flourishing industry in America, with manufacturers producing what are known as "knock-offs" in the "rag trade". Of course, the quality of cloth was difficult to mimic – especially the limited-edition fabrics designed by Rodier of France, hand-woven exclusively for him by peasant women in Picardy. In the case of French designer Madeleine Vionnet, the cut and seaming arrangement of her garments was impossible for anyone else to understand, and so were difficult to copy exactly.

These fashions demanded special accessories. And so shoes and handbags of matching fabrics or complementary colours would be ordered for each outfit. Teams of fine craftspeople specialized in various aspects of the accessory trade. For instance, Paris-

Walking advertisements: this pair of British girls have the answer to runs and holes – the major stocking problem of the decade once hemlines reached the knee.

based Ugo lo Monaco included hand-painted feathers and silk flowers in his embroidery. Carlo Piatti of Como, Italy, was renowned for embroidered silk shawls.

Cutting Corners

Mass production was made possible by a variety of factors: the modernization of the factories, mainly through electrification, and the economical, tubular cut of women's wear. Simplicity of shape meant efficiency – a

Unusual Values

16 X 220
Crepe
$4.98

16 X 225
Embroidered
"Har'd Twist"
Voile
$8.98

16 X 221
Embroidered
Voile
$5.98

22 X 3091
Hand-
Embroidered
Voile
$2.79

16 X 224
Imported
Ratine
$6.98

16 X 222
Figured
Crepe
$2.98

16 X 223
Pure
Linen
$7.49

Stylish Dresses at Moderate Prices

See Opposite Page for Descriptions and Other Colors of These Charming Dresses
DO NOT DELAY YOUR ORDER BY FORGETTING TO GIVE SIZE AND COLOR DESIRED

Page 31

American mail order fashions featured in *The National Style Book*, published in New York in 1924.

Sewing Goes Electric

In the 1920s electricity revolutionized housework and factory production alike. For example, a new generation of sewing machines, each powered entirely by a small electric motor, went into production. The implications for home dressmakers, as well as machinists in clothing factories, were enormous. In the 1920s middle-class women were the main target of the electrical household revolution; the first features to be electrified were lighting and water heating, and then came the first of those consumer goods that most homes take for granted today. In 1921 the Women's Engineering Society in Britain held a competition for the invention and improvement of labour-saving devices for the home. Two years later, the American company Frigidaire brought out an electric ice box, the forerunner of the refrigerator.

A study of one British store gives some idea of how fashion for women was filtered down from the model gowns of Paris to the paper patterns used by home dressmakers. Following its redecoration in 1920–24, Bon Marché – calling itself "Liverpool's Modern Store" – offered three types of service, in addition to ready-made garments. The most exclusive service was that of the Model Gown Salon on the second floor, which catered to traditional custom-made ("bespoke") dressmaking. The floor below housed an inexpensive dressmaking department, where the customer could choose a paper pattern and a length of cloth from the nearby fabric department. These could then be made up in the store's workroom, and the cost

saving of time and energy. The loose, modern fit meant that dresses could be manufactured in a standardized range of sizes, requiring minimal adjustment to the individual figure. Although mass production made the latest fashion accessible to a much wider range of the buying public, there was still a big difference between haute couture and simple home dressmaking from paper patterns. Even so, they were connected. To bridge the gap, in the 1920s certain Parisian couturiers began to sell original models wholesale; Jean Patou was one of the first to do this.

14

would include one fitting. The next department offered a cut and fit service; here the customer could buy the pattern and necessary materials, and the store's workroom would cut, baste (sew loosely) and fit the garment, to be sewn and finished by the customer at home.

As happens today, paper patterns were modified versions of the *toiles* (pattern pieces cut out of calico) devised by the houses of established couturiers. Like the new clothing factories, they helped to make fashion more accessible. McCall's, an American pattern manufacturer, promoted the latest styles for the home dressmaker through a film, in which mannequins modelled the garments made up from their patterns.

Despite mass production, the expansion of retail services and growth in the numbers of women sewing at home, the independent professional dressmakers were still in demand, especially for wedding dresses. Although many of them set up shops or workrooms, others, especially in England, operated on the same basis as the old Victorian sewing ladies, who would visit the house for a specified period of time, to make up or alter garments as required by the female members of the household.

The New Consumer

The new consumerism did not just mean a revolution in what was being manufactured, but in how the new products were marketed. America led the way: promotional feature articles appeared in women's magazines of the 1920s under titles like "Best Dressed Products Sell Best".

As we have seen, mass production coincided with more uniformity of design and standard sizing. An efficient system of garment construction was clearly argued in the manifestos written by Soviet fashion designers following the Revolution of 1917 and subsequent civil war in the Soviet Union, where political rather than financial

motivation spurred the clothing factories into action.

Consumerism – at least according to manufacturers and retailers – was the key to emancipation and democracy. The sales war in cigarettes exploited the female market – women were coaxed into smoking, to "prevent sore throats" or as an aid to losing weight. Many brands offered collectable pictorial cigarette cards, a cheerful surprise for the children (a single card was tucked inside each package), and this put pressure on mothers to go out and buy more packages to make up the set.

Window shopping became a new pastime in the decade. The introduction of plate glass made the paned windows and colonnades of Victorian and Edwardian department stores look very old-fashioned. In the 1920s window displays featured clothes worn by life-size, flesh-coloured dummies,

Evening coat made of an exotic fabric in silk and lamé, designed by Raoul Dufy, 1927. The straight-cut coat gives a slender silhouette and the wide sleeves accentuate slim hips – as well as making it easy to slip over an evening dress.

painted with realistic hair and make-up. But occasionally, something more novel or abstract could be found; in Paris, fashion accessories were sometimes displayed on dolls with painted cloth-covered faces, one of these being based on the famous cabaret singer Mistinguette.

Once enticed inside the store, life was made as easy as possible for the modern shopper. For example, mass production of clothing necessitated some uniformity, which led to a new, rational sizing system. It also sorted customers into more clearly defined "types", according to income bracket

Three Snap
All Rubber
GAITER

RITZ
IMPERIALS

— or, in the case of Bullock's Department Store in Los Angeles, six personality types. These were: the Romantic, the Statuesque, the Artistic, the Picturesque, the Modern and the Conventional. The Modern type was:

The fashionable type. The woman who can fit herself into the latest mould without discomfort. Just now shingle-bobbed. Boyish. Sleek. Skirts short when they are so. And longer than anybody's when they are so.

On the other hand, the Artistic type was:

A bit enigmatic. Usually with a suggestion of the foreign. Usually dark-haired, dark-eyed. A type that may accept vivid colours, bizarre embroideries, eccentric jewellery. The artistic type welcomes the revivals of Egyptian, Russian and Chinese motifs and colourings. Peasant necklines. Berets. Hand-loomed fabrics.

The new consumer responded to modern technology, including new forms of communication. Of course, fashion magazines continued to be an important source of ideas and information, and in the twenties these grew in number and variety; many articles focused on aspects of modern life, such as the new sports and the clothes that went with them. The link between Hollywood and fashion developed toward the end of the decade, and certain styles were christened with the names of the film stars who wore them.

Advertisement for Ritz Imperials, rubber foot protection by Firestone – available in black, gunmetal or mocha brown – designed to slip over smart evening shoes, 1929.

American film star Clara Bow with kohl-rimmed eyes and cupid-bow lips – christened the "It" girl, because she definitely had "It" (i.e. sex appeal).

P755-37

Hy. Fournier

Le black-bottom au faubourg

Aquarelle de Henry Fournier

The Age of the Machine

Post-war modernism brought about admiration of the machine. This involved a belief that new materials, mass production and a degree of automation could improve the quality of life. This idea was expressed in twenties' transportation, architecture and fashion alike. For instance, the work of American car manufacturer Henry Ford, Swiss architect Le Corbusier (Charles-Edouard Jeanneret) and French designer Coco Chanel were all radical in their different ways, for ignoring excessive detail. Ford's functionalism was motivated by a desire to reach the mass market. To designers like Le Corbusier and Chanel, the clean, simple lines and efficiency of the machine inspired a sense of beauty that could be suggested through the pure function of materials carefully chosen for the design in hand.

This "machine aesthetic", as it is known, was expressed through all the visual arts in a variety of ways. The jerky movements of dances such as the Black Bottom, Texas Tommy, the craze for jumping on pogo sticks, the angular, stylized acting in silent movies, and the wearing of dresses with a metallic finish, all seemed to echo the machine. In 1924 *Vogue* featured scarves, as stiff as propellers, tied into "airplane bows", and Chanel's steel beads; in 1927 shiny patent leather shoes were described as "new". This metallic influence was expressed in the robots of Fritz Lang's film *Metropolis*, in 1926.

"Le Black Bottom", as danced in Paris. Like the Charleston, the dance was introduced into Europe by professional black entertainers from the United States.

Just the thing to be seen in at Palm Beach – a smart but casual three-piece suit, along the lines of Coco Chanel's knitted jersey fashions. Designed by the house of Worth, 1921.

The shape of things to come? Robot from Fritz Lang's film *Metropolis*, 1926.

Sport for All

The twenties innovations in sport and exercise make an impressive list: calisthenics (a form of gymnastic exercise), squash, mechanical horses, rowing machines, massage by wide electric belt and, last but not least, the "medicine ball" (an enormous beach ball). The youthful, healthy minded search for sun and sport among the rich was heralded by the optimistic symbol of the rising sunburst – a popular motif of later Art Deco style. With the new building programme and the growth of suburbs, municipal golf courses, swimming pools, football stadiums and other sports facilities were opening up, making leisure activities available to greater numbers of people. At the Olympic Games of 1924 and 1928 "the greatest swimmer ever" came home with a handful of gold medals and world-beating records. His name was Johnny Weissmuller – though he was to become better known as Tarzan for his film role.

Time and motion studies were not just applied to machines in the modern factory, but to the human form. A doctor friend of Le Corbusier wrote an article called "The New Body" in the avant-garde journal L'Esprit Nouveau in 1922. Dr Pierre Winter announced:

Sport brings an element of order into life . . . It demands the demolition of outworn frameworks. It introduces the law of balance which governs work and repose. It imparts precision and coordination to our movements. It trains us in quick reactions. It gives the time factor its fitting place in modern life.

The machine was also the key to mass manufacture, to the democratization of fashion. The Soviet Constructivist artist Varvara Stepanova, who was involved in designing textiles and clothing in the post-Revolutionary spirit of the 1920s, stated in 1919:

Today's dress must be seen in action – beyond this there is no dress, just as the machine cannot be conceived outside the work it is supposed to be doing . . . Aesthetic aspects must be replaced by the actual process of sewing. Let me explain: don't stick ornaments onto the dress, the seams themselves – which are essential to the cut – give the dress form. Expose the ways in which the dress is sewn, its fasteners, etc., just as such things are clearly visible in a machine.

And so in the 1920s fashion blended with the world of industrial design. In industry, the "American system" had

"Matches and Match Boxes", an American printed dress silk designed from a photograph by Edward Steichen, and manufactured by the Stehli Silk Corporation, c. 1928.

been established by the mid-nineteenth-century. It involved the mass production of standardized products, constructed from interchangeable parts. Each of these parts was made using power-driven tools, in a sequence of simplified mechanical operations. This "simplicity in multiplicity" was essential to achieve maximum efficiency.

The division of labour was considered a necessary part of production in this new machine age. Although his shoes were still being made by hand, Italy's Salvatore Ferragamo decided to change the organization of his workshop to improve efficiency. Whereas before, the cutting of the vamp (the front part of the shoe's upper), the piecing together and stitching of the various parts had all been done by one person, Ferragamo decided to assign each individual task to separate craftspeople. In Paris, Madeleine Vionnet built an American factory behind her private mansion in the Avenue Montaigne. Her work force of about 1000 employees was treated to the healthiest facilities; a dispensary and dental clinic were attached to the workrooms, where a ventilation system changed the air at three-minute intervals. (Immunization was only beginning to happen in the 1920s, and for many years clothing was recognized as a common source of infection because the fabric could harbour germs.)

Fashion and the Arts

The Jazz Age, as it has been dubbed, spread from the United States to Europe in 1919, when the all-white Original Dixieland Jazz Band, which had created such a sensation in Chicago and New York three years previously, opened a three month season at the Hammersmith Palais de Danse in London. Playing by ear (for not one musician in the band could read music), their spine-tingling notes on trumpets

Illustrator Thayaht matches the intricate cut and machine-like precision of this tailored autumn outfit by Madeleine Vionnet with his own mechanical style, 1923.

and saxophone attracted a full house every night, before going on to tour around Europe. But in most people's minds, jazz was associated with New York City's Harlem renaissance, or revival, of black arts in the 1920s.

The black stage show, the "Revue Nègre", came to Paris in the 1920s, at the same time that jazz was taking off. Star of the revue, black American Josephine Baker, sparkled in white society, entertaining fashionable people with her exotic costumes and performances. Wearing her famous banana costume or covered in tropical plumage, she interpreted the "African" vogue with the sounds and dances of jazz. There are many descriptions of her ". . . a woman possessed . . . a shining machine à danser, an animal, all joint and no bones . . ." one moment the fashion artist's model, the next Picasso's. They all underline white society's romantic view of non-European cultures.

This general enthusiasm for black and other non-European cultures was reflected in the new exhibitions in Paris at the time. The Musée de l'Homme (Museum of Mankind) and smaller galleries displayed the art of Africa, for the benefit of avant-garde artists and collectors alike. In 1922 an exhibition of African art from the French colonies featuring tribal masks and sculpture took place. Three years later the Galérie Ritlinger staged an exhibition of Indonesian art from the islands of Java and Bali, which coincided with the fashion for batik (a technique of patterning textiles by drawing on the design in wax before dyeing).

Paris was the international centre of culture and experimental art. Artists and writers from many backgrounds

Orientally inspired evening gowns in rich lacquer-red, by Worth, 1923. The lavish embroidered panels of diamanté and coloured silks were crafted by specialized workshops that served the exclusive fashion houses of Paris.

and nationalities came together to soak up the avant-garde atmosphere. Many settled there; others stopped off to perform on their European tours. The names of new art movements were quickly picked up by the fashion designers and applied to printed dress fabrics, which could be called "Futurist", "Cubist" or "Surreal". Although some of these works, like Serge Diaghilev's productions of the

Poster by August Trueb advertising a Haid and Neu sewing machine, embodying the spirit of the machine age, 1928.

Russian Ballet, were first enjoyed before the war, they were still reflected in the colours and forms of the decorative arts popular throughout the twenties.

23

There was a fruitful mixing of ideas from many different art forms in the Paris of the twenties. For example, Russian ballet impresario Diaghilev staged a production of the ballet *Le Train Bleu* in 1924, for which artist Picasso designed the backdrop curtain and fashion designer Chanel's sportswear of jersey fabric was the basis of the costumes. Not only did fashion artists take inspiration from painters – Italian-born Elsa Schiaparelli from Spain's Surrealist Salvador Dali, for instance – but the great couturiers, notably Jacques Doucet, were among the leading art patrons of the day.

In fashion illustration, artist Erté created fantastic effects in stage and costume design for France's Folies Bergères, and later for America's Ziegfeld Follies. He also illustrated covers for *Harper's Bazaar*, while the cover of *Vogue* bore the art of Georges Lepape, Benito and occasionally artists such as Giorgio De Chirico who did not specialize in fashion illustration. During the first half of the decade, drawing was the main means of communicating fashion ideas, and some of the most colourful and stylish illustrations were produced by the *pochoir* process (a method of stencilling). Some of the finest examples can be found in the exclusive French journals *La Gazette du Bon Ton* and *Art Goût Beauté*.

Fashion photography was a new challenge that appealed to avant-garde photographers but was being used to surreal effect, rather than as an accurate record of the latest designs available. As the decade progressed, more and more photographers became interested in fashion. The chief names of the medium are Edward Steichen and Man Ray, Baron Gayne de Meyer, George Hoyningen-Huene and Cecil Beaton. Steichen and de Meyer were enormously influential in the early years, working in succession as chief photographer for American publisher Condé Nast (de Meyer left for Hollywood and was then employed by *Harper's Bazaar*). London-based Beaton created theatrical effects, devising various painted or paper cut-out backdrops for his portraits of society women. In 1925 Hoyningen-Huene joined *Vogue* in Paris, but broke away from the confines of the studio into the open air – capturing aspects of metropolitan lifestyle or a bird's-eye view of bathers on a beach. Experimenting with lighting and playing with differences of scale, Man Ray evoked the surreal quality of fashion itself; in 1929 he was joined in this way of working by fellow-American Lee Miller – the first woman to make an impact in the world of fashion photography.

Nightclubs

By the late twenties Josephine Baker's success led to the opening of her own nightclub in Paris. She would arrive in her chauffeur-driven Voisin car, its brown body and snakeskin upholstery exactly matched to the colour of her skin. The effect of her dramatic entrance was captured in *Vogue*:

> She had come in without a wrap, and the length of her graceful body . . . is swathed in a full blue tulle frock with a bodice of blue snake-skin . . . her hair, which naturally grows in tight curls, is plastered close to her head with white of egg and looks as though it were painted on her head with black shellac. As she appears at the Folies Bergères, she wears only a diamanté maillot of tulle and red gloves with diamond balls hanging from the tips of her fingers; the effect is up to the wildest imagination of Beardsley.

Several of London's nightclubs were run by the famous hostess Mrs Meyrick. And in New York City's Harlem, white society frequented the jazz clubs where great musicians such as Louis Armstrong, Duke Ellington and Cab Calloway entertained. The most famous of these spots was the Cotton Club. Recalling the late 1920s,

The First "Talkie"

"Wait a minute. You ain't heard nothin' yet!" were the first words spoken on screen – by Al Jolson in Warner Brothers' *The Jazz Singer* in 1927. The previous year, Warner Brothers produced a film with synchronized music recorded on discs – a system called Vitaphone. Silent movies had been accompanied by the movie-house piano or organ, the player changing the music's rhythm and mood to suit the action on screen. But with the arrival of "talkies," dialogue took the place of the piano and the exaggerated gestures, costumes and sets of the silent movies. The story no longer depended on fast-moving slapstick and caricature, whether in Felix the Cat cartoons or the comedies of Fatty Arbuckle or the clownish but sad Charlie Chaplin. As the decade progressed, cowboys and Indians were increasingly featured.

this personal memory of Sonny Greer conjures up some of the atmosphere:

> We went to work at 11 o'clock at night, and nobody knew when closing hour was. We usually didn't get through till seven or eight in the morning, but it was beautiful . . . all kinds of people mixed there – show people, socialites, debutantes, musicians and racketeers – and everybody had a lovely time. It was still Prohibition . . . nobody could get a drink of booze in the place unless I gave an okay . . . The last show at the Cotton Club went on at two and the club closed at 3:30 or four. Then everybody would go next door . . . or to the breakfast dance at Small's Paradise, where the floor show went on at 6 o'clock in the morning.

Sometimes black musicians were hired to play in private Manhattan apartments or country homes, but colour barriers were rigidly kept and white and black audiences did not mix. Though jazz was thought of as an expression of black culture, there were also white American jazz bands that attracted huge crowds – for instance, the Original Dixieland Band, and entertainer Paul Whiteman, whose orchestra was the first to perform "Rhapsody in Blue" in 1924, with the composer George Gershwin at the piano.

The Wall Street Crash

October 1929. Virtually overnight, the fortunes of many Americans, who were just getting used to their massive spending power, came crashing down. Big profits led to wild speculation, causing the prices of stock shares to rise above their true value. The resulting "slump" and panic were inevitable. The dramatic fall in prices affected the rest of the world's stocks and shares and led to mass unemployment. With the stock market crash, the hemlines of women's dresses also dropped. As often happens, an air of seriousness and "playing it safe" went hand in hand with the economic crisis.

The almost identical Hungarian Dolly Sisters, international entertainers. Here pictured performing in London's exclusive Kit Kat Club.

The vamp, with her kohl-rimmed eyes, exotic Egyptian dress and oriental decor is as typical of the twenties as the lover of sun and snow in her worsted tunic and breeches.

Flappers

Thoroughly Modern Millies

Undeterred by the disapproval of adults, the younger generation was setting out to have a good time. The emancipated female painted her face and drank cocktails. She smoked cigarettes placed in elegant holders. She might wear a Turkish-inspired "smoking suit" and turban. Her boyish silhouette is sometimes referred to as the "garçonne" look – all flat-chested beneath the new shapeless fit and revolutionary brassière. To achieve the new slim line – modern, minimal, geometric – the surface of the body was broken up by shapes of contrasting colour, dismantled and reassembled rather like a Cubist painting by Picasso or Braque.

By 1925 dresses were the shortest in history – an act of the devil, some thought. There was an international outcry to protect the moral code; here and there campaigns were launched to save the future generation from chaos and destruction. What's more, legs were given the impression of nudity, thanks to the flesh-coloured stockings of artificial silk, which women of all income levels could afford. The American states of Ohio and Utah responded by passing laws fixing the hem length at around seven inches from the floor – but legislation such as this usually exempted girls below the age of 14, still regarded as innocent children.

Taking it easy in a smoking suit, 1922. The texture of the fur ankle trim contrasts with the luminous surface of the artificial silk textile – as well as the cigarette holder. A turban adds to the exotic effect – and seems appropriate for smoking Turkish or Egyptian cigarettes.

Colour and Form

For much of the decade dresses and sweaters were pure rectangles – like canvases waiting to be painted. And in fact, several artists became involved in dress and textile design. In Paris, Sonia Delaunay created colourful abstract compositions in fabric and fur. Collaborating with the furrier Jacques Heim, she made a coat this way, plus matching seat upholstery for her brightly painted Citroën sports car. In Vienna, members of the Wiener Werkstätte (Viennese workshops) created fascinating stylized floral decorations for hats out of sculpted and sewn pieces of felt – they made innovative cloth necklaces, too. Soviet artists, on the other hand, designed nothing so frivolous or decorative; the painters Popova and Stepanova applied Constructivist principles to everyday dresses, making dynamic use of red.

Opposition in Dress

Just as hemlines rose, the emphasis on women's legs was matched by the voluminous dimensions of "Oxford bags". These broad trousers, worn by undergraduates of Oxford University, were a cool – but dishevelled – response to the hot British summer of 1925. Looking back on his own experiences as an Oxford undergraduate at that time, the British aesthete Harold Acton described them as a localized Victorian Revival, worn with "high necked jumpers [pullovers] of all tints and textures." Like England's most prestigious universities, Oxford and Cambridge, Ivy League undergraduates in the Northeast enjoyed a relaxed mood in dress – blazers and flannel trousers, cravats rather than ties – that broke away from the conventions of the three-piece suit. Other, less prestigious American colleges saw their men adopting distinctive ways of dressing. Sharp-brimmed hats, racoon fur coats, and two-toned "saddle shoes" were just some of the choices. Fraternities flourished, each identified by a particular code of dress.

Colour, texture, looser and lighter-weight clothes had gone hand in hand with progressive thinking before World War I. In his bohemian days, the American poet Ezra Pound had worn a green jacket trimmed with glass buttons. In the twenties, these elements gradually entered fashion; young men's clothes looked very colourful compared to the khaki and grey of their parents. They wore lounge suits with jackets when in town, instead of knee-length frock coats. Their trousers were creased front and back, and turned up at the ankle, while conservative dressers stayed with side creases and straight legs of narrower cut. New men about town were clean shaven, instead of bearded.

Short Back and Sides

One of the most persistent features of the twenties was the cloche hat, worn by women to tea dances, in the street and even at lunch parties in their own homes. This head-hugging hat was as storm-proof as a flying helmet. It necessitated a short hairstyle called a bob, a shingle or an Eton crop – thus, before the decade had run its course, 99 per cent of the American and Western European female population had their hair cut short.

The heroine of Scott Fitzgerald's short story of 1920, "Bernice Bobs Her Hair", fascinates her friends at parties by talking of bobbing her hair. When she actually strides into a barber's and has it done, she is immediately rejected by her horrified young companions for looking so ugly.

Miss Kitty Lee, society girl of Baltimore, Maryland, with a portrait of her boyfriend printed onto her stockings. With the new short hemlines of the mid-1920s, it was difficult to hide the stocking tops.

Simply Shocking!

The legendary escapades of Britain's Bright Young Things included revelries such as a Babies' Ball, in which a reckless young fashionable elite got drunk wearing rompers, pinafores and sailor suits, and raced around fashionable London squares in baby buggies. Another "madcap" idea of fun was to crash parties – and there were plenty of them. Everyone enjoyed song and dance and dressing up. And in the United States the "Jazz Babies" were fascinated by scavenger (i.e. treasure) hunts. But the twenties were a time when shock and outrage were touched off far more easily than today. A scarlet, backless evening gown was enough to do the trick.

Cloche hats with love symbols. For the initiated, the tying of the ribbon carried a coded message: arrow-like, it indicated the single girl who had already given her promise of love; the firm knot meant she was married; but a flirtatious bow was the symbol of the independent, fancy-free girl.

F. Scott Fitzgerald and his wife, Zelda, on their honeymoon in 1920, casually dressed in tweed and wool jersey.

"That frock's so short you can see your garters", a postcard by Donald McGill. Garters came in all textures and shades – often trimmed with metallic beads or colourful embroidery, they were meant to attract attention.

A youthful party in Paris; *Art Goût Beauté*, Christmas issue, 1923. The young men are formally dressed, but with a neckline softened by large floppy black bow ties – something Oscar Wilde might have worn. The four women in the foreground (left to right) wear evening gowns by the Paris fashion houses of Molyneux, Philippe et Gaston, Lucien Lelong and Bernard.

for Economical Transportation

CHEVROLET

$\mathcal{S}$UPERLATIVELY SMOOTH in its operation, the new Chevrolet Six stands high among the most ably engineered cars in the world. And it is this thoroughness of engineering, with fine workmanship, that has made Chevrolet the overwhelming choice of those who instinctively seek a quality product . . . closed bodies by Fisher.

CHEVROLET MOTOR COMPANY, DETROIT, MICHIGAN
Division of General Motors Corporation

The Roadster, $525; The Phaeton, $525; The Coach, $595; The Coupe, $595; The Sedan, $675; The Sport Cabriolet, $695; The Convertible Landau, $725. All prices f. o. b. factory, Flint, Michigan

SIX IN THE PRICE RANGE OF THE FOUR!

For economical transportation, Chevrolet – advertisement featured in American *Vogue*, 1929.

The Perfect Gentleman

American Dreams

Travel became easier and more accessible through the decade. Transatlantic exchanges of ideas entered everyday life – including clothing. Novelist F. Scott Fitzgerald's high-living, high-spending Jay Gatsby, of the novel *The Great Gatsby,* embodied the aspirations of those men for whom success meant good dress. As Gatsby opened "two hulking patent cabinets which held his massed suits and dressing gowns and ties, and his shirts, piled like bricks in stacks a dozen high," he explained that a man in England sent him clothes every season, spring and fall. His admirers looked on in amazement as he pulled out shirts "of sheer linen and thick silk and fine flannel . . . and the soft rich pile mounted higher – shirts with stripes and scrolls and plaids in coral and apple-green and lavender and faint orange, with monograms in Indian blue."

In New York, the Brooks Brothers men's store was the place to go for traditional dressing – America's equivalent of Savile Row in London. Meanwhile in Chicago, the press reported on gangster Al "Scarface" Capone who paid attention to detail in everything that he touched. That included his spats, his showy necktie, his fob watch and chain tucked into his waistcoat pocket, his distinctive pin-striped suits – and, of course, the brimmed felt hat worn at an angle designed to cast a shadow over the scar on his cheek.

Prince of Wales Checks

Edward, Prince of Wales, heir to the British throne, looked elegantly dressed in a checked lounge suit when he visited Texas cowboys in 1919. He admired the casual, open-necked shirts and style of Americans, and whenever he could he introduced elements of sportswear and country clothing into his own dapper wardrobe. He loved fast cars and riding and preferred the ease of a knitted sleeveless pullover sweater to the tailored waistcoat beneath his hunting coat. He also enjoyed golf. In 1922, when playing the game at St. Andrews, Scotland, he sported a brightly knitted Fair Isle pullover sweater – worn with plus fours, also known as knickerbockers – which attracted public attention, drew in many orders for the Hebridean Island knitters, and became a best-seller. *Vanity Fair* magazine regularly featured the Prince of Wales in its "Well Dressed Man" column. London's Bond Street and Savile Row led the world in men's fashion, and he was their greatest ambassador.

The Prince of Wales wearing a Fair Isle pullover, which he wore with knickerbockers for playing golf. He started a fashion for this Scottish knitwear.

"Stop Flirting"

American dancer Fred Astaire's first London performance, in *Stop Flirting*, was a huge stage success in 1923. When the prince visited him backstage, Astaire was impressed:

HRH [the prince] was unquestionably the best-dressed young man in the world, and I was missing none of it. I noted particularly the white waistcoat lapels – his own special type. This waistcoat did not show below the dress coat front. I liked that.

The following morning, he paid a visit to Hawes and Curtis, shirt- and waistcoat-makers By Appointment to the Prince. Then, the royal outfitters ruthlessly protected their clients, unlike today, when Harrison Ford's famous Indiana Jones hat comes from the same Bond Street hatters as Prince Charles's. The dancing star was politely turned away from Hawes and Curtis, and had to go elsewhere to follow the best-dressed man's style.

Getting It Right

Despite the liberalism of the day, there remained a strict sense of etiquette that taught a young man what was permissible and "correct". No "gentleman" ever showed his braces or shirt sleeves. Nor would he mismatch a hat and coat – Homburgs and straw hats should not be worn with evening dress, whereas caps belonged to work wear and sports clothing. The gestures that went with them – raising hats and doffing caps – were signs of social distinction, especially in Europe, where class and social conventions were more clearly defined than in the United States.

Fashionable French couple walking in the Bois de Boulogne, Paris, 1921. With great flair, the man wears a striped shirt with plain white collar (detachable), tweed jacket and pin-striped pants, and spats – an unconventional combination that no American or British man would ever have dreamed of.

The Prince of Wales riding with the cowboys in Texas,
c. **1920 – obviously a spontaneous gesture, because he is wearing a suit (normally he would wear riding breeches and knee-high boots for riding).**

Known as ''Oxford bags,'' these wide-leg trousers entered fashion in the summer of 1925, worn by young undergraduates at Oxford University.

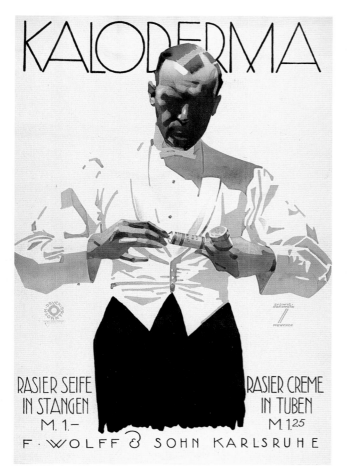

German advertisement for Kaloderma shaving cream, 1929. The stiff-winged collar, white bow tie and white pointed waistcoat are all features of the most formal, conventional evening dress for men – to be worn with top hat and tails.

Gentlemen raising their hats to passing acquaintances in a park. The suit, worn with double-breasted waistcoat and double-breasted overcoat, was by French tailors Lus and Befue, 1922.

Colourful printed silk fashions by Sulka for men with dash – and cash – the kind of accessories that poured out of Jay Gatsby's wardrobe, described in *The Great Gatsby*.

Stars of Stage and Screen

Sparkle and Glamour

Motion pictures began life as an inexpensive form of escapism, available to a far wider audience than the theatre or ballet. In terms of dress, the medium had immense power – especially in the silent early years, when sharply defined costume and gestures were essential to the narrative. Black-and-white movies called for strong tonal contrasts in the clothes worn by the stars; the sparkle of beads and metallic finishes, and the movement and texture of feathers, could be picked up dramatically by the camera.

On stage, too, the quality of light made people look at colour in a different way. In 1927 the British menswear trade journal *Tailor and Cutter* approved of the midnight blue evening suit worn by the star of André Charlot's revue *A to Z*, Jack Buchanan, because it looked much better under electric light than did conventional black. Buchanan had the ideal physique to promote the broad-shouldered suit introduced to fashion by Savile Row in 1925.

The film heroes of the decade were altogether as smooth and unblemished as the female stars, since the negatives were touched up to perfection. Rudolph Valentino, labelled "The Sheik" after one film role in which he depicted a romantic desert prince, caused women to swoon in their seats, though to our eyes he may appear decidedly over made-up and downright camp, with his highly brilliantined hair looking like patent leather. On the other hand, Tarzan (alias U.S. Olympic Gold swimmer Johnny Weissmuller) was flexing his muscles with charisma – but looking very unreal compared with

The heart-throb of the silent screen until his tragically early death in 1926. Rudolph Valentino – perfectly made up, with slicked back hair.

the authentically clothed cowboys like Gary Cooper who first appeared in the thirties.

Vamps, Virgins and Femmes Fatales

Recently described as the forerunner of today's well-tailored woman, Louise Brooks's independent, tomboyish style matched the office dresses and suits she wore in films. These widely influenced the viewing public. Lillian Gish, on the other hand, was cast as the pure maiden – dressed, inevitably, in white; her sugary-sweet image was not a fashion sensation.

The vamp, exemplified by stars such as the hypnotic and seductive Theda Bara, whose eyelids glistened with vaseline, was another female type that had entered the movies during World War I. Titles such as *Sinners in Silk* took the opportunity to show off ''prostitute pink'' camiknickers of silk or rayon. Among the other *femmes fatales* to be ''discovered'' by German and American film directors were: Pola Negri, Gloria Swanson, the great Greta Garbo – and Clara Bow, known as the ''It Girl''. ''It'' meant sex appeal. An American dress fabric, printed all over with the word ''it'', was designed by Ruzzie Green in 1928.

Not all of these stars wore silk pyjamas – but those who did were generally considered ''fast'', i.e. of loose morals. In the Gershwin musical comedy *Oh, Kay!*, which opened on Broadway in 1926, the English star Gertrude Lawrence wore such an outfit. The silk was encrusted with pearls, the matching open robe seductively trimmed with ostrich plumes, which wafted from the sleeves. For her stage and film appearances she was dressed by the Paris house of Molyneux for nothing, because the publicity for them was invaluable. In France, another star of musical comedy, Yvonne Printemps, wore Jeanne Lanvin garden party dresses, together with picture hats – very romantic and escapist in the age of the machine and the tubular cut.

Hollywood Clothes Horses

Once the movie industry was centred on Hollywood by the end of the 1920s, its glamour was limitless, and the star-studded screen became a focal point around the Western world for the spread of fashion ideas. The response of the Paris couturiers was to hire American models to show their collections every autumn and spring. Several couturiers entered Hollywood, to design for the movies – but although Coco Chanel's designs for ballet costume were superb on stage, her garments were too understated to make an impact on screen. Hollywood designers Howard Greer and Travis Banton, however, had worked in the fashion business before entering the film industry, and they had a good understanding of what was photogenic. On the other hand, shoe designer Salvatore Ferragamo first attracted fashionable customers by making sandals for the film *The Ten Commandments* (1924). Paris and Hollywood had all the makings of a perfect alliance.

Greta Garbo and John Gilbert dressed for their parts in *Flesh and the Devil* of 1927. She always looked mysterious, often veiled as in this picture. His knitted mohair overcoat is worn over a high-collared jacket.

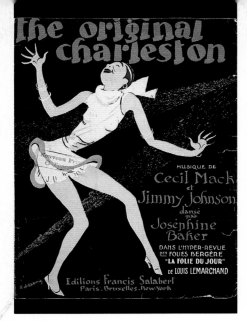

Josephine Baker, the black American dancer and singer, depicted on a French sheet music cover of 1923.

Richly coloured silk dressing gowns were the idle luxury of the rich, for lounging around in at home. Noel Coward loved wearing them – and did so in his play *The Vortex*, 1924.

Gypsy-looking Vilma Banky, the cover story of *The Picturegoer*, November 1926.

Pola Negri covered in shimmering lamé.

THE NOVEMBER

Picturegoer

MONTHLY

1926

Vol. 12
No. 71

1/ net

Vilma Banky
SPECIAL
ARTICLE
INSIDE

Chic Parisienne

Great Couturiers

Throughout the twenties, the well-established fashion houses – such as Callot Soeurs, Jacques Doucet, Lucile (Lady Duff Gordon), Paul Poiret and Worth – continued to create exciting garments, heavily embroidered and intricately constructed from beautiful fabrics. However, Coco Chanel, Madeleine Vionnet and Elsa Schiaparelli broke new ground in the cut and concept of clothes, responding through their designs to broader movements in modern art.

Rich Little Poor Girl

Impressed by work clothes and the comfort of men's cardigan sweaters worn by women who took over men's jobs in the factories during World War I, Chanel combined simplicity with elegance. She favoured rough tweeds and other work-wear fabrics, making it fashionable to look poor. She also devised dresses and two-piece outfits made from Rodier's wool jersey. Her collections featured numerous variations on the sweater theme for day-wear. Many of her geometric designs were inspired by Scottish Fair Isle and Icelandic knitting, with their jigsaws of pattern and colour. The little black dress and edge-to-edge coat (in which side fronts meet, with no fastening or overlap) are also attributed to her. And Chanel's influence led to the popularity of frankly fake jewelry – including long ropes of artificial pearls.

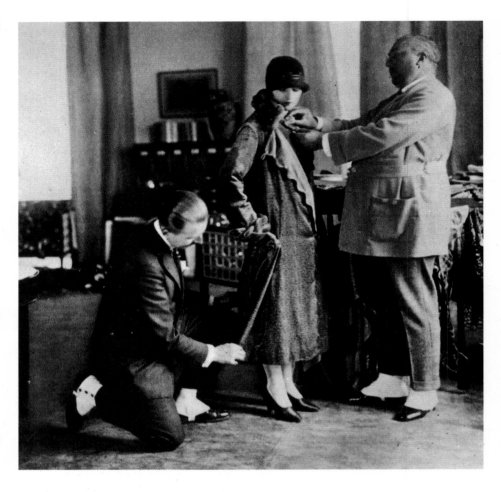

Paul Poiret with his tailor, fitting a model dress on a "mannequin".

The Art of Deception

Chanel's greatest rival was the Italian-born Elsa Schiaparelli, famous for the incongruous elements she introduced into her designs. Schiaparelli was much influenced by Salvador Dali and the Surrealist movement. To her, dress designing was not a profession but an art, which should always treat the body like an architectural frame, with respect. Yet she was frustrated by the force of fashion, for many of her original ideas were copied in mass production. In her autobiography *Shocking Pink* she wrote: ". . . as soon as a dress is born it has already become a thing of the past . . . A dress cannot just hang like a painting on the wall, or like a book remain intact and live a long and sheltered life."

Schiaparelli's clothes were always expensive, beautifully cut and incredibly chic – but whimsical. Around 1926, her first fashion hit was a *trompe l'oeil* (literally, "fool the eye") sweater, in which the image of a huge bow was hand-knitted into the design. The garment finished at the natural waist, in complete contrast to the straight, tubular silhouette of that time, which emphasized the hips. Immediately, a buyer from the New York store Strauss ordered 40, with matching skirts. This success led to many more deceptive sweaters – designs taken from artifacts of the Congo, a knitted simulation of a sailor's chest tattooed with pierced hearts and snakes, and a skeleton of white ribs against a black background. Schiaparelli also had some silk printed with a montage of fake newspaper clippings all about herself – one of the first puns on the "designer label" idea. This fabric was used for men's ties. Schiaparelli's exciting colour sense found expression in a whole range of fashion accessories, and she experimented with new cloths, textures and finishes – for example, white rubberized crêpe for women's flying outfits in 1928.

On the Bias

Most of the tube-shaped dresses followed the straight grain of the fabric. But Vionnet's inventive clothes, which were cut on the bias from the shoulders and hips, were so fluid and perfectly sculpted, using heavy satin and crêpe. The cut gave the garment an in-built elasticity. It was possible to step into one of her low-backed evening dresses with no hooks, ties or other fastenings. As well as long evening gowns in understated tones of oyster and pastel blue, and other draped dresses for wearing in the afternoon, she designed tailored suits and capes for outdoor wear in town. Like Chanel, Vionnet never sketched her designs; she always worked in three dimensions, letting the fabric dictate, preferring tucks to cuts. She draped the cloth around a wooden model, measuring a quarter of human size, which stood on a revolving piano stool.

Latest Paris fashion at the Grand Prix motor race, June 1924.

Boutiques and Branches

During the decade, several new names sprang up, and although Paris remained the centre of high fashion, the whole scene diversified and turned more international. For example, American Hattie Carnegie, who had launched her first collection in 1918, added ready-to-wear models ten years later, following the footsteps of Paris's Lucien Lelong. Some designers opened boutiques in fashionable resorts, targetting their garments at a specific clientele, and lent their names to perfumes, as Paul Poiret had begun to do just before World War I. Schiaparelli led the field in creating colourful accessories – handbags, shoes and even wigs for skiing – to match her outfits. And in 1926 Jeanne Lanvin opened the first boutique for men, to complement her clothes for women and children.

"What! Already dressed?" – evening gown and silk pyjama outfits by Jeanne Lanvin, 1924.

Evening gown of heavy silk satin with low, draped back, *c.* 1924, designed by Madeleine Vionnet.

Diamanté-studded shoe designed by Pérugia. Long ropes of pearls, sometimes looped into a knot, were draped seductively to draw attention to bare skin – preferably sun-tanned.

Rich silks, black and white embroidery, and monkey fur collar trim in an evening gown and cape designed by Paul Poiret.

Tutmania and All That Jazz

Tutmania

The discovery of the ancient Egyptian king Tutankhamen's tomb in 1922 sent the world spinning into a frenzy of "Tutmania". Egyptian motifs entered many areas of the fashion market. Colours were christened with names like Coptic blue, sakkara, Egyptian green and carnelian. Cheney Brothers, the American textile company that produced stylish hand-printed dress silks, sent out a designer to Egypt to seek first-hand inspiration. Hieroglyphs and motifs that looked like a cross between an Art Deco sunburst and Cleopatra's headdress covered fashion accessories, from handbags to enamelled cigarette holders and even "mummy" powder compacts.

Panels of embroidery in hieroglyphic patterns inspired by ancient Egypt, incorporated into Walpole's smart overblouse of 1923.

Ancient Egypt was suddenly popularized through cheap imitations of "Cleo" earrings and scarab-shaped jewelry; and the lotus motif became the logo of a brand of footwear.

North Africa also influenced fashion, but in a more general sense. Black cotton net stoles from Morocco, decorated with twisted strips of silver arranged in geometric patterns, were popular in this period. They created the sort of dazzle that black-and-white movies encouraged. Women bathed their bodies in iodine baths to tint the skin a reddish colour. Brilliantly offset by this effect or by a tan, ropes of pearls looked stunning. Many women used kohl as eyeliner, to accentuate the eyes in a vampish manner.

Rhythms and Patterns of Jazz

The jerky and syncopated rhythms of jazz, and dances like the Black Bottom and the Charleston that went with them, were echoed by the hard-edged patterns of dress fabrics. To create maximum impact on the dance floor, corsetless flappers were free to move, and their loose-cut dresses swivelled around them. In time with the fast beat of the music, fringes swung wildly, and the dresses, heavily decorated with glass beads, dazzled brilliantly under sharp electric light. In 1925 Josephine Baker and the "Revue Nègre" arrived in Paris, at a time when the poet Nancy Cunard — wearing a mass of African ivory bangles up her arm — was living in the city with her black jazz musician lover, Henry Crowder.

"Primitivism"

The "primitive" appealed to the new machine-driven, urbanized world. As a result, in the competitive mass-produced world of fashion, a rich variety of decorative motifs was borrowed from many cultures. These included the rhythmic stepped patterns of South America's Pre-Columbian ceramics and tapestries, stylized floral borders of East European folk embroidery, and the triangles of West African cloths. Batik was also in fashion — and had the advantage of being simple to experiment with at home, especially for those women who got hold of a manual on the craft by artist Jessie M. King (1922) called *How Cinderella Went to the Ball*. The French painter Raoul Dufy designed hundreds of textiles for the Lyons silk firm Bianchini-Férier; many of these took the theme of the jungle, and other exotic images.

Fashions for the Orient

The impact of the *Thousand and One Nights*, expressed in Paris through Diaghilev's Russian Ballet production of *Schéhérazade* in 1910, continued to resound well into the twenties — especially in the field of colour, and the rich textures of Turkish velvet and brocade. And although Paul Poiret's turbans and pantaloon gowns had faded from fashion, the love for Oriental styles lived on in timeless classics. Historic and exotic themes were interpreted in a very individual way by Mariano Fortuny, the Venice-based dress and textile designer.

The Callot Soeurs (of Russian ancestry) lavished upon their creations Chinese-style embroideries in the colours of painted porcelain – worked into birds of paradise and lotus flowers. The skills of their needlewomen were also invested in details around the knee-length hem – tassels, scallops and lavish beading – which drew attention to the legs. Japanese style, too, was enjoyed; the decoration of T-shaped kimonos was easily translated into peasant-inspired Art Deco coats, overlaid with apple blossoms, bamboo and mythical phoenixes.

Norman Hartnell evening fashion for 1924, trimmed with metal bead embroidery and ostrich plumes.

"Visit Egypt" – 28 days of luxurious
travel for only £72 10 shillings.
British *Vogue*, October 1929.

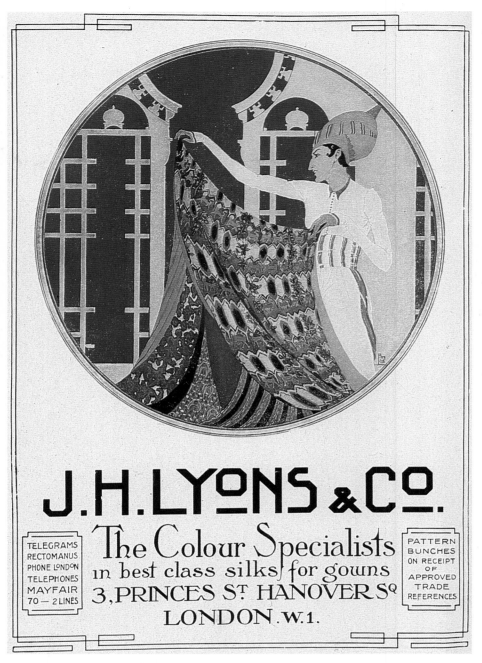

Silks offer an amazing variety of
exotic colour and textures in this
advertisement for the fabrics of
J. H. Lyons and Co.

Lawrence of Arabia

A German silver and cloisonné enamel brooch of the 1920s; the scarab was a popular motif under the influence of "Tutmania". It was considered to be a sacred beetle in ancient Egypt and used as decoration in precious stones for jewelry.

Writer Nancy Cunard (for some time Paris correspondent of American *Vogue*) wearing African bangles, with her black jazz musician lover Henry Crowder. They shocked the establishment by openly living together.

McCallum's silk hosiery, advertised in American *Vogue*, December 1921.

Annie Ondra in sensational costume – flesh-coloured silk camiknickers – in the first British "talkie", *Blackmail*, 1927.

Strong, light and practical
"Hercules" roller printed cotton
manufactured by Joshua Hoyle & Co.
Ltd, of Manchester.

Jane Régny clothes for yachting,
1928; a suit of white serge unbuttons
quickly to reveal a slinky white
jersey bathing costume underneath,
embroidered on the pocket with the
"JR" monogram.

In Search of Sun and Sport

Elasticity in Action

One of the biggest influences on fashion has been sport. In the 1920s barriers were being broken down between these two fields of dress. Coco Chanel revolutionized day wear and sportswear alike by creating casual suits and golfing outfits of jersey that had "elasticity in action" and "slender lines in repose".

Golf fell into the category of traditional sports, so golf clothing, like that for riding and fishing, tended to be made of older-fashioned heavier cloths, such as tweed and plaid. The conservative nature of the fabric was echoed by the restrained cut of the golfing skirt – i.e., inverted pleats that did not swing round the body so widely as to set the wearer off balance.

Skiing and flying – belonging to the new generation of sports – demanded flashy metallic detail, dazzling snow white, or the colours nearest to primary available. Waterproof, yet pliable, ski mittens were made of chromed (i.e., leather with a metallic finish) horsehide. Buckles and zippers were used experimentally as outer details on the most dynamic of sportswear, in which the component parts were assembled, only to be detached and rearranged to perform a new function and create a new silhouette within seconds. For example, in 1926 the house of Redfern (which had turned international, following its nineteenth-century origins at Cowes, Isle of Wight, making yachting clothing) designed a skating outfit of white velvet – apparently one-piece, but the skirt of which zipped off to become a scarf.

Amateur Athletics

The French financed the first European meeting of women athletes, held in Monte Carlo in 1922. The athletes – all amateurs in those days – wore black woollen stockings, white cotton pullovers (a bit like today's sweatshirt), black "drawers" (bloomers) and mottled grey and black plimsolls. They did not have the range of white leather sneakers we do today.

Anyone for Tennis?

In London, Wimbledon's Centre Court was the focal point of radical sportswear that hit the headlines, and was soon picked up by tennis enthusiasts around the world – both off court and on. Men still wore long trousers for tennis, but in 1926 the Duke of York set a precedent at the Lawn Tennis Championships by wearing "sleeves cut short above the elbow". Consequently, from then on, "no other man need be afraid to do so", assured the Sunlight League's Dr Saleeby.

In women's tennis, French champion Suzanne Lenglen caused a sensation with her chic wardrobe of tennis dresses designed by Jean Patou. She was instantly recognizable by the coloured bandeau, wound round her head, matching her monogrammed sleeveless cardigan. The low-cut neckline of the dress featured an ingenious lapel that could be buttoned up to the neck after the match – at which point, Lenglen stepped into another casual but impeccable Patou ensemble, looking little different from on court.

Another tennis star to attract the imitators was America's Helen Wills, famous for her eyeshade. Together, she and Lenglen changed the future of tennis, for their less restrictive clothes sped up the game. Nevertheless, modesty and convention demanded that they continue to wear white stockings – baring the legs was a freedom and privilege restricted to the fashionable scene of the seaside resort.

From Riviera to Palm Beach

A suntan was once the rough and ready sign of a peasant worker. But during the twenties it acquired a sense of refinement. Those who had sufficient wealth and time on their hands to travel abroad paraded the decks of their yachts or the esplanades of the new seaside resorts. Pages of *Vogue* featured the Palm Beach and Riviera styles – beach trousers and backless bathing suits. These originated in the Paris couture houses, but could be bought in the growing number of boutiques catering for this leisured outdoor life under the sun. For instance, Charles Worth opened boutiques at Biarritz and Cannes, two of France's most fashionable resorts. And in America, the West Coast became a centre for outdoor fashion by the late 1920s – to be boosted by the Hollywood phenomenon in the next decade.

British photographer and fashion chronicler Cecil Beaton recalled the personification of "a new type of woman", in the beautiful form of a Spanish duchess:

> . . . wearing a short white tunic with a deep scooped neckline and a skirt that stretched hardly to the knees. She wore sunburn stockings with white satin shoes whose Spanish spike heels were fully six inches high . . . she was burned by the sun to a deep shade of iodine. Two

enormous rows of pearl teeth were bared in a white, vital grin, complementing the half a dozen rows of pearls as large as pigeon's eggs that hung about her neck.

"Bathing beauties in Plymouth", shading themselves from the sun under a beach umbrella with design inspired by the artist Raoul Dufy. (In fact, this was a set-up studio shot.)

Sportswear for the beach, on sale in the Paris department store Les Grands Magasins du Louvre in 1929; the influence of Coco Chanel is felt strongly in these outfits – especially the three-piece suit with geometrically patterned sweater.

Winter sports clothing in "agnella", a woven wool fabric resembling sheepskin, designed by Rodier.

Practical sports clothing designed by the Soviet artist Varvara Stepanova, 1923. In the 1920s Soviet fashion made dynamic use of the colour red and political images like the hammer and sickle.

A carefree beach dress in chevron-patterned lightweight wool by the great French textile designer-manufacturer of the decade, Paul Rodier.

French tennis star Suzanne Lenglen, sporting a Jean Patou outfit at the Wimbledon lawn tennis championships; she delighted the crowds and was champion from 1919 to 1923 and again in 1925.

Cross-dressing was part of the whole process of dress reform and political emancipation for women; it also was taken up by fashion designers, as shown in this mannish golfing outfit.

Rich, strong, vibrant colours in loud checks and stripes, for travelling clothes. Wearing these colours in the street was considered extremely eccentric.

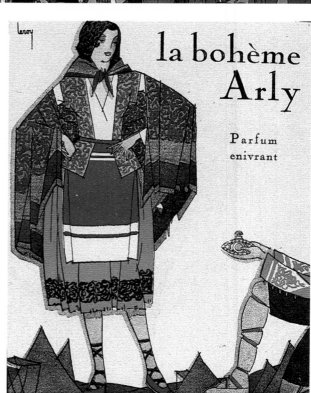

la bohème Arly

Parfum enivrant

Dare to be different! Arly's intoxicating perfume will make you feel like the bohemian you truly are! This kind of costume was still being worn by peasants in Eastern Europe and Scandinavia and was the inspiration for many alternative, artistic dressers in the 1920s.

Man or woman? The gender of the figure in the centre, wearing formal black-and-white evening dress for a man, is only detectable by her shoes.

Members of the Men's Dress Reform Party, founded in London in 1929, wearing the shorts, loose collars and soft, lightweight colourful fabrics (including velvet and silk chiffon) for which they were ridiculed more often than praised; after all, if women could now expose their knees and wear looser clothing, why shouldn't they?

Glossary

Art Deco A geometric style of decorative art. The term was coined from the Exposition des Arts Décoratifs et Industriels Modernes, Paris, 1925.

Avant-garde (French for vanguard) Supporting or expressing the newest ideas and techniques in an art.

Batik A textile onto which the design is drawn in wax before dyeing.

Bauhaus German school of art and architecture, founded by Walter Gropius in 1919, forced to close under the Nazis in 1933.

Bianchini-Férier Lyons textile firm. Through 1920s produced printed and woven fashion fabrics including designs by French painter Raoul Dufy.

Callot Soeurs Three sisters of Russian ancestry who in 1890s set up Paris fashion house. Exotic evening dresses combining Chinese motifs, lavish embroidery, plumes, lace and antique textiles.

Carnegie, Hattie American designer who assembled her first fashion collection in 1919 – neat gray worsted suits, straight skirts, jeweled buttons were her hallmark. In 1928 she launched ready to wear collections.

Chanel, Gabrielle ("Coco") (1873–1971) French designer, established in the Paris couture business by 1919. Known for simple, functional garments of wool jersey, inspired by menswear and working dress – especially sweaters and pleated skirts. Recognized the importance of sportswear, put the little black dress on the map, and encouraged the fashion for costume jewelry.

Constructivism Dynamic, very exact, non-representational style of art bridging art and industry that originated in Russia.

Cubism Movement in painting seeking to represent several aspects of the same object (or group of objects) viewed from different angles within one composition, using cubes and other solid geometrical figures. In its purest form in works of Georges Braque and Pablo Picasso *c.* 1910–1912. Later, other Cubisms are experimented with, and the term is applied to some geometric decoration.

Delaunay, Sonia (1885–1979) Brought up in Russia, studied drawing in Germany and painting in Paris. She made her first "simultaneous" paintings in 1912 and in the 1920s she translated this abstract art into fabric and fashion designs.

Diaghilev, Serge (1872–1929) Russian, a member of the artistic and literary circle of St. Petersburg. Created the Ballets Russes, which first performed in Paris in 1909. Dancer Vaslav Nijinsky, designer Leon Bakst and composer Igor Stravinsky were stars of Diaghilev's pre-World War I productions. In the 1920s he commissioned artists like Sonia Delaunay and Pablo Picasso to design sets and costumes for new ballets.

Erté (Romain de Tirtoff: 1892–1990) Russian-born fashion illustrator and designer of fantastic sets and costumes for the Folies Bergères revues in Paris, and later their American equivalent, the Ziegfeld Follies. In the 1920s he created stunning evening dresses for Mrs. William Randolf Hearst, wife of the American publishing magnate.

Ferragamo, Salvatore (1898–1960) Innovative Italian shoe designer and manufacturer, who made a name for himself in Hollywood, then set up company in Florence, Italy in 1927.

Fortuny, Mariano (1871–1949) Spanish, but working in Venice from 1907, painter and stage designer as well as creator of textiles and dress. Designed simple garments with rich fabric effects and details such as lace and eyelet fastenings weighted with Venetian glass beads. Took inspiration from Classical, Medieval and Islamic statues and decorative arts. In 1920s opened shops in London and Paris.

Futurism Art movement claiming to anticipate or point the way to the future. Futurist artists created a feeling of dynamic motion in their works.

Haute Couture Most expensive sector of the fashion industry, in which clothes directly based on "model" garments are custom made.

Lanvin, Jeanne (1867–1946) French couturier, well known by 1915 for romantic "robe de style" inspired by dresses designed for young girls. Opened boutique for men's clothes in 1926. Responsible for installation of Pavillon d' Elégance at the 1925 Art Deco exhibition.

Lelong, Lucien French couturier. Opened fashion house 1923. Created models for his wife, the society beauty Princess Natalie Paley, who publicized his style.

Lepape, Georges (1887–1971) One of the leading French fashion illustrators.

Lucile (Lucy Wallace Duff Gordon) (*c.* 1870–1935) Canadian born, first London-based fashion designer of international repute. Claimed credit for liberating women from corsets and introducing new bright colors. Sister of romantic and sensationalist novelist Elinor Glynn, who may have inspired Lucile's dress titles such as "Sweet sounds of lips unsatisfied." Lucile also designed luxurious lingerie.

Molyneux, Edward British, trained by Lucile. Set up his own establishment in Paris in 1919 creating classic clothes of restrained elegance.

Patou, Jean (1880–1936) French couturier involved in fashion design from 1914. Formed his own establishment in 1919. One of first Parisian couturiers to market wholesale copies of original models. Renowned for his smart sportswear, tennis champion Suzanne Lenglen wore JP outfits on and off court.

Poiret, Paul (1879–1943) Worked with Paris houses of Doucet and Worth before opening his own salon in 1904. Created clothes of simple cut, brilliant colors and rich textures. The first couturier to introduce perfume. He extended design from clothes to interior decoration, with the Atelier Martine, the opposite of the machine aesthetic. His influence waned during the 1920s and exhibitions located in barges on the Seine at the 1925 Paris exhibition were a financial disaster.

Post-Impressionism Art movement following Impressionism, aiming to express the spiritual quality of things, rather than a realistic representation of their physical appearance.

Rodchenko, Alexander (1891–1956) Russian Constructivist involved in socially useful applications of art after the 1917 Revolution – especially graphics and photography.

Rodier French company founded by Paul Rodier, said to have produced 5000 textile designs per year for innovative and exclusive haute couture fabrics, mostly in wool and linen. He employed cottage hand weavers in Picardy.

Schiaparelli, Elsa (1890–1972) Born in Rome, Schiaparelli developed reputation as fashion designer in Paris from *c.* 1928, when she introduced hand-knitted trompe l'oeil sweaters. Famous for her witty and colourful use of decoration, fastenings and accessories, she was in the vanguard of new fashionable silhouettes, e.g., broad shoulders *c.* 1930; much work inspired by Salvador Dali and the Surrealist movement.

Surrealism From *c.* 1919, a movement in French art and literature that sought to draw on the subconscious, escaping the control of reasoning or preconception.

Vionnet, Madeleine (1876–1939) French designer who was apprenticed in a fashion house at age 12. Worked for Doucet and Callot before opening her own house in 1912. A pioneer of the bias cut, using it by 1920 for cowls, necklines and handkerchief dresses.

Worth The first great couture house, founded in Paris in 1858 by English-born Charles Frederick Worth (1826–1895), later run by his sons and grandsons. There were branches in all major capitals of Europe by 1900. Worth dressed royalty and created very dignified clothes.

Reading List

Many books have been published on the 1920s and on fashions in the decade. Magazines and movies are also excellent sources of information.

Attfield, J. and Kirkham, P., *A View from the Interior: Feminism, Women and Design*, The Women's Press, 1989.
Baines, B., *Fashion Revivals*, Batsford, 1981.
Battersby, M., *The Decorative Twenties*, Studio Vista, 1969.
Bowman, S., *A Fashion for Extravagance*, Bell & Hyman, 1985.
Byrde, P., *A Visual History of Costume: The Twentieth Century*, Batsford, 1986.
Carter, E., *The Changing World of Fashion*, Weidenfeld and Nicolson, 1977.
Charles-Roux, E., *Chanel and Her World*, Weidenfeld and Nicolson, 1984.
Etherington-Smith, M., *Patou*, Hutchinson, 1983.
Evans, C. and Thornton, M., *Women and Fashion*, Quartet Books, 1989.
Forty, A., *Objects of Desire: Design and Society 1750–1980*, Thames and Hudson, 1986.
Hall, C. (ed.), *The Twenties in Vogue*, Octopus, 1983.

Hall-Duncan, N., *The History of Fashion Photography*, Alpine Books Company, New York, 1979.
Hardyment, C., *From Mangle to Microwave*, Polity Press, 1988.
Heskett, J., *Industrial Design*, Oxford University Press, 1980.
Hillier, B., *The Style of the Century 1900–1980*, E. P. Dutton, New York, 1983.
Jarvis, A., *Liverpool Fashion: Its Makers and Wearers*, Merseyside Museums Service, 1981.
de Marly, D., *The History of Haute Couture 1850–1950*, Batsford, 1980.
de Marly, D., *Fashion for Men*, Batsford, 1985.
O'Hara, G., *Encyclopaedia of Fashion*, Thames and Hudson, 1986.
Osma, G. de, *Fortuny – Mariano Fortuny: his life and work*, Aurum Press, 1980.
Robinson, J., *The Golden Age of Style: Art Deco fashion illustration*, London, 1977.
Steele, V., *Paris Fashion: A Cultural History*, Oxford University Press, 1988.
Vreeland, D., *Inventive Paris Clothes 1909–1939*, Thames and Hudson, 1977.
Whitford, F., *Bauhaus*, Thames and Hudson, 1984.
Williams, B., Portrait of a Decade: The 1920s, Batsford, 1989.

Wilson, E., *Adorned in Dreams: Fashion and Modernity*, Virago, 1985.
Wilson, E. and Taylor, L., *Through the Looking Glass*, BBC Books, 1989.

Some novels written in or about the 1920s

Arlen, M., *The Green Hat*, 1924.
Fitzgerald, F. Scott, *This Side of Paradise*, 1920; *The Great Gatsby*, 1925.
Forster, E.M., *A Passage to India*, 1924.
Hemingway, E., *A Farewell to Arms*, 1929.
Huxley, A., *Chrome Yellow*, 1921; *Antic Hay*, 1923; *Point Counter Point*, 1926.
Joyce, J., *Ulysses*, 1922.
Lawrence, D.H., *Women in Love*, 1921; *Lady Chatterley's Lover*, 1928.
Lee, L., *Cider with Rosie*, 1959.
Lehmann, R., *Dusty Answer*, 1927.
Lewis, Sinclair, *Main Street*, 1920.
Maugham, W. Somerset, *The Painted Veil*, 1925.
Priestley, J.B., *The Good Companions*, 1929.
Waugh, E., *Decline and Fall*, 1928; *Vile Bodies*, 1930; *Brideshead Revisited*, 1945.
Woolf, V., *Mrs Dalloway*, 1925; *Orlando*, 1928.

Acknowledgments

The Author and Publishers would like to thank the following for permission to reproduce illustrations: The Mary Evans Picture Library for pages 11, 14, 19, 22, 30c, 35b, 47b, 49b; The Hulton Picture Company for pages 7b, 9, 10b, 12, 28, 29, 35, 41, 49a, 51b, 53, 56; Lighthorne Pictures for pages 10a, 12, 15, 16, 18, 21, 23, 31a, 35c, 38a, 41b, 42a, 46a, 50b, 54b, 58a, 58b, 59a; Popperfoto for page 36; Publisher's archives for pages 17, 25, 32, 37, 40; The Vintage Magazine Co. for pages 2, 6, 7a, 8, 20, 26, 27, 31b, 35a, 39, 44, 46b, 51a, 54c, 55a, 57, 63. The illustrations were researched by David Pratt.

Time Chart

NEWS	EVENTS	FASHIONS
20 Prohibition begins in USA League of Nations has its first session	First radio broadcasts French tennis star Suzanne Lenglen wins Wimbledon for second year running Charlie Chaplin's first full-length film, *The Kid*	Chanel's pioneering jersey sweater and pleated skirt ensembles are now accepted easy wear Debutante Daisy Fellows challenges convention wearing black when presented to the Queen at Buckingham Palace instead of the traditional white
21 Lenin introduces new economic policy in Russia Partition of Ireland First birth control clinic founded by Marie Stopes	Expansion of public sports grounds, golf courses, etc. Albert Einstein awarded Nobel Prize for physics; his *Theory of Relativity* is published	*Dress Essentials* magazine features scarves among accessories; colour co-ordination becomes a conscious feature of the average woman's wardrobe
22 America's first female senator Mussolini becomes the first Fascist dictator in Europe Mahatma Ghandi imprisoned for taking an anti-British stance USSR formed	Fleet Street newspaper "circulation war" in London American Johnny Weissmuller (the original Tarzan) is first man to swim 100 metres in under a minute Egyptian boy king Tutankhamen's tomb discovered	The Prince of Wales now orders all his trousers to be made with turn-ups, and (unlike his father) wears lounge suits in town East European folk embroideries inspire the peasant look in women's wear
23 Collapse of Deutschmark gives rise to protesting factions, including Nazis Ku Klux Klan reign of terror in America Progress in public health: tetanus and diptheria immunization introduced	First full-scale exhibition of Bauhaus work; Schlemmer's *Mechanical Ballet* is performed	Soviet Atelier of Fashion is formed Bobbed hair becomes the rage Tutmania takes off with "Tutankhamen" overblouses, Egyptian colors, scarab and lotus jewelery, etc.
24 Passenger air travel begins British Empire Exhibition held at Wembley Olympic Games, Paris	Noel Coward's play *The Vortex* is staged in London George Gershwin composes *Rhapsody in Blue*: orchestrated jazz Paris fashion and arts meet in Diaghilev's *Le Train Bleu* ballet: stage curtain by Picasso, sportswear by Coco Chanel Michael Arlen's *The Green Hat* is published	The Textile Colour Card Association of the United States is formed: an attempt to establish a standard system of colours identified by numbers
25 Hitler's *Mein Kampf* published Britain returns to the Gold Standard Cocktails from America are taken up by smart society in Western Europe New homes are being installed with electricity	Art Deco exhibition held in Paris Charleston and Black Bottom arrive in Europe, taking over from the waltz and fox trot Louis Armstrong forms the Hot Fives jazz band F. Scott Fitzgerald's *The Great Gatsby* is published	*Vogue's* first feature on the "little black dress" "Oxford bags" are worn by young graduates The hemline is the shortest in history U.S. production of rayon viscose reaches 53 million pounds for the year
26 General Strike in Britain Death of Rudolph Valentino Modernization/Westernization in Turkey Scotsman John Logie Baird demonstrates the first successful television system to scientists in London	Fritz Lang's film *Metropolis* is released Margaret Kennedy's novel *Constant Nymph* is published A. A. Milne writes *Winnie the Pooh*	More masculine elements enter female dress The severely short "Eton crop" haircut ousts bobbed hair Jeanne Lanvin opens first boutique for men
27 American Charles Lindbergh makes first solo flight across the Atlantic Freestyle, barefoot dancer Isadora Duncan is killed Kuomintang takes Shanghai, afterward Red Army is set up in China	Warner Brothers make the first "talkie", *The Jazz Singer*, starring Al Jolson Henry Seagrave exceeds 200 mph in land speed bid	Patent leather and fish skin shoes are new Nancy Cunard, wearing African bangles to the elbows, is photographed by Man Ray
28 "Flapper vote" is made law in Britain Indian National Congress demands Dominion status for India Stalin launches Five Year Plan; Trotsky is exiled Herbert Hoover becomes U.S. President	D. H. Lawrence's *Lady Chatterley's Lover* banned in Britain Mickey Mouse created, to join Felix the Cat in Walt Disney's menagerie	The press declare "fever chart" hemlines Hat brims return to fashion The first of Schiaparelli's trompe l'oeil sweaters are a resounding success
29 Wall Street Crash St Valentine's Day Massacre, Chicago Second Labour Government in Britain; first woman cabinet minister appointed Arab-Jewish rioting in Palestine Graf Zeppelin makes a round-the-world flight	Salvador Dali makes his first surrealist film, *Un Chien Andalou* Kodak produces first 16 mm colour photographic film (but popular box cameras still restricted to black and white)	Men's Dress Reform Party is founded in Britain A new femininity: hemlines are now longer for daywear, as well as evening

Index

Figures in *italics* refer to illustrations.